Dogs and Puppies

Katherine Starke

Designed by Kathy Ward
Edited by Fiona Watt

Illustrated by Christyan Fox
Photographs by Jane Burton
Cover design by Amanda Gulliver
Additional research by Jonathan Sheikh-Miller

CONTENTS

Consultant: Barry Eaton
With thanks to Andrew Kirby

Choosing a dog

It's a good idea to look at lots of different dogs before you choose one. Animal shelters and vets are a good place to start looking. If this is your first dog, you may find it easier to get a puppy rather than an adult. You will need to train a puppy, but most of them learn quickly. A puppy is ready to leave its mother when it is about 6-8 weeks old. Check that the puppies' mother is friendly. Her puppies will probably be friendly too.

This German Shepherd Dog is 8 weeks old.

These Spaniels are 12 weeks old.

Picking a puppy

Choose a dog that will not be too big for your house.

Choose a friendly puppy.

Before you choose a puppy, try to find out as much as you can about its parents. If they are big, then their puppies will be big too.

If you can, play with the puppies for a while to see what they are like. Look for one that likes people, as well as other dogs.

Pick a puppy that is not bossy and not very shy. A bossy puppy may be hard to control and train when it grows up.

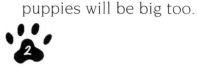

For a link to a website where you can learn
about many different types of dogs, go to
www.usborne-quicklinks.com

Types of dogs

Dogs that have been bred to look and act a certain way are known as purebred. If you choose a purebred puppy, you will be able to find out how big it will grow and what sort of dog it will be.

Purebred dogs may need special care, such as extra grooming or lots of exercise. They can cost a lot of money to buy. Find out as much as you can about the breed before you buy a purebred dog.

This Labrador Retriever is a purebred puppy.

Dogs come in lots of different shapes, sizes and fur types.

Other dogs are a mixture of different breeds. It is more difficult to guess what a mixed breed puppy will be like and look like when it grows up. Mixed breeds can be healthier and live longer though than some purebred dogs.

Labrador Retrievers, like this puppy, are usually friendly, but need lots of exercise.

What will I need?

Before you bring your dog home, you will need to get a few things for it. It will need some toys, something to sleep in, some food and food dishes, and something to travel in when you bring it home. Make sure that you have everything ready before your new dog arrives.

Pet carrier

If you are getting a small puppy, it is safest to use a pet carrier to take it home. Ask if you can borrow a carrier from the person selling your puppy, or from a vet.

This is a plastic dog carrier but you can get carriers made from cardboard.

Toys

Your dog will need some toys to play with when you are not there. Look for special dog toys that are safe for it to chew.

Somewhere to sleep

Find a cardboard box that is big enough for your dog to lie in. Cut a section out of the front. Make sure that the front is low enough for your dog to climb in.

Put the bed in a warm, quiet place.

Put some newspapers in the bottom and an old blanket inside to make it snug. If you have a puppy, you will need to change its box for a larger one as it grows.

For a link to a website where you can answer a range of questions
to find out which type of dog suits you best, go to
www.usborne-quicklinks.com

Collar and tag

Your dog will need a collar and an identity tag in case it gets lost. Put your name and telephone number on the tag. When you put a collar on your dog, make sure that you can get two fingers between the collar and your dog's neck. If you have a puppy, check every few days that its collar is not too tight. Buy your puppy a bigger collar as it grows.

This tag has the owner's name and telephone number inside.

Something to eat

Your dog will need a dish for food and one for water. Put the dishes in a quiet place, where your dog will not be disturbed as it eats.

SNIFF...
SNIFF...

Put some newspaper under the dishes.

Buy a small amount of food at first, in case your dog doesn't like it. Food with 'complete' on the label will have all the things your dog needs to eat to stay healthy.

5

First days

When you bring your dog home for the first time, it may be excited and nervous. If you get a puppy, this may be the first time that it has left its mother. There will be lots of things that seem very strange to it. Keep your dog in just one or two rooms for the first few days, so that it can get used to its new home.

Talk quietly to your dog so that it will get used to your voice.

First things first

Put some food in the dish and tap it to show your dog where it is.

When you bring your dog home, try not to make lots of noise. It may be scared or nervous to start with. Show your dog its food dish. It may be hungry.

Puppies get tired very quickly.

Let your dog explore its new home, but stay with it. Leave your dog to go to sleep if it wants to. It may be tired after exploring its new home.

Making friends

Say your dog's name and hold your hand out for it to sniff. Crouch down so that your dog can see your face better. Try not to look directly into your dog's eyes.

Stroke it gently along its head and back.

Your dog will think that you want to fight if you stare at it.

Meeting people

When you take your dog for walks, it will meet different people. So that this won't seem strange, get your dog used to meeting people as soon as you can.

Let it meet just a few people at a time at first.

Shhh!

Your dog may cry at night to start with, but it will soon get used to being on its own. Wrap a hot water bottle in a towel and put this in your dog's bed for it to cuddle up to.

A puppy will need more sleep than an adult dog.

Don't wake your dog if it is asleep.

Settling in

Your dog will need time to get used to its new home and other animals you have. If you have a puppy, it will need injections before you can take it out (see page 17). Dogs can catch diseases from places where other dogs have been to the toilet. You will need to clear up any mess your dog makes. Page 22 tells you how to clear up when you are out for a walk with your dog.

At night, put a thick layer of newspaper near your puppy's bed, where it can go to the toilet.

House training

If you have a fenced area outside, take your puppy out to go to the toilet. Do this after meals, after it has been asleep, and after you have played with it.

Watch for signs that your puppy needs to go out. It may sniff the ground and crouch down.

Stay outside with your puppy until it has finished. If it goes to the toilet, make a fuss of it, to show that it has been good.

For a link to a website where you can ask a vet about any problems your dog might have settling in, go to
www.usborne-quicklinks.com

Clearing up

Wear rubber gloves and pick up any mess with an old spade. Wrap it in a plastic bag and throw it away, then wash your hands well. Dog mess can make you very ill.

Meeting other pets

When your pets first meet, let them sniff each other.

SNIFF...
SNIFF...

Before your dog meets a cat or another dog, put some of its bedding near your other pet's bed. This lets your other pet get used to the smell of your new dog.

It is best to wait for several days before your dog meets any other animals you may have. Don't let it meet small pets, such as rabbits or mice. It may try to chase them. If your other pet is a cat, keep your dog on a leash for the first few meetings. If your pets try to fight, take your new dog away. Keep the first meetings quite short.

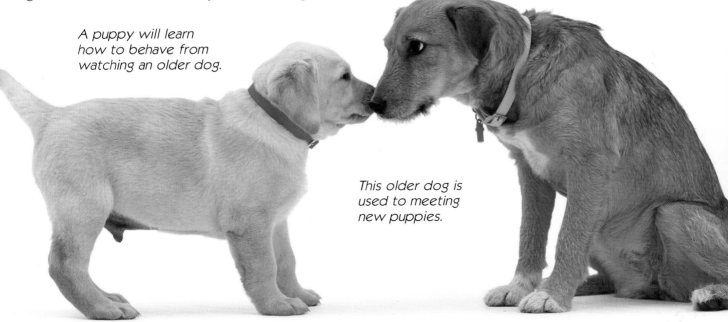

A puppy will learn how to behave from watching an older dog.

This older dog is used to meeting new puppies.

Feeding

A dog likes to be left alone when it is eating, so put its food and water dishes in a quiet place. If you have another dog or cat, feed your pets away from each other. They may try to steal each other's food.

It's best not to play with your dog just after it has eaten. Let it rest for a while, so that it does not get an upset stomach.

A plastic food dish, like this one, won't tip over as your dog eats.

Types of food

Feed your dog ready-mixed dried or canned food. Special puppy food has extra things in it to help your puppy stay healthy.

How much?

Different-sized dogs need different amounts of food.

Find out how much your dog weighs to figure out how much to feed it. The label on your dog's food will say how much it needs.

Weigh your puppy by getting it to sit down on a set of bathroom scales. Do this every week until it is about six months old.

For a link to a website where you can try out
some tasty recipes on your dog, go to
www.usborne-quicklinks.com

Feeding your dog

*Use an old spoon to put
food in your dog's dish.*

If you have a puppy, feed
it four small meals a day.
This is better than feeding
it a lot of food in one meal.

Fill a different dish with
cold water. Make sure your
dog always has fresh water
in its dish.

At six months old, give
your dog two meals a day.
When it is fully grown, feed
it one or two meals a day.

Bones and chews

Most dogs love to chew
bones or dog chews.
Chewing also helps your
dog to clean its teeth.
Never give your dog bones
which have been cooked,
or chicken bones. They
might splinter as it chews
them and hurt your dog's
mouth. Give it uncooked
bones instead. You can
buy these from a butcher's
or a pet store.

*Give your dog a
bone, or a dog
chew like this
one, as a treat.*

Playing

Dogs love to play games with other dogs, toys and people. Puppies like to play even more than dogs and can be boisterous. They play to exercise but also for fun. Buy your dog several different toys so that it does not get bored with them. You can buy special toys for dogs from pet stores. These are tougher than ordinary toys.

Play biting

These puppies are play-biting.

They bite each other very softly.

Puppies often pretend to fight and bite when they are playing. This is known as play biting. They don't hurt each other when they do this.

Watch out for teeth

OUCH!

If your puppy bites you as you are playing with it, say "Ouch!" in a loud voice and stop playing. Teach your puppy that you won't play with it if it is too rough.

I want to play!

Your dog might show you that it wants to play with you. It drops its head down onto its front paws and puts its bottom up in the air. This is called a play bow.

For a link to a website where you can print out
and make 3-D models of all sorts of dogs,
go to www.usborne-quicklinks.com

Playing with your dog

*When your dog
shakes a toy, it
is pretending
to kill it.*

Roll a ball for your dog to
chase. Use one that's larger
than a tennis ball, so that
your dog can't swallow it.

Play hide and seek with
your dog. Hide behind a
piece of furniture and call
your dog's name.

Always give your dog a toy
to play with when you're
not there. A rubber dog toy
is good for it to chew.

*This spaniel
puppy is rolling
a squeaky toy
with its foot so
that it makes
a noise.*

*Its tail is wagging to
show that it is happy.*

13

Dog language

Your dog uses different movements and noises to tell you what kind of mood it is in. It might bark when it wants attention and growl when it wants to be left alone.

When you meet any dog for the first time, watch it carefully to see if it is friendly or not. Ask the owner's permission before you touch their dog.

Roll over

Your dog may wag its tail when it is happy. It may also lift its ears up and draw its lips up, as if it is smiling. It may lift its head up to show that it wants to play with you.

When a dog rolls over and shows its stomach, it is saying that it trusts you. Most dogs like to have their stomachs scratched.

This puppy's ears show that it is happy.

Feeling scared

When a dog is scared of something, it tries to look as small as it can. It tucks its tail between its legs and flattens its ears against its head. It may also crouch down and creep away.

Your dog might do this if another dog tries to fight it.

A dog will not look you in the eye if it is nervous or scared.

Curious dog

Dogs prick their ears up so that they can hear better. A dog might do this if it sees or hears something interesting. It sits still and tips its head to one side, waiting to see what will happen next.

Go away!

If a dog barks at you, it may be telling you to go away.

When a dog defends itself, it shows its teeth and crouches down, ready to spring if it needs to. It flattens its ears against its head and may bark.

Keep clear!

Be careful when you go near a dog that you don't know.

When a dog gets angry, it growls and shows its teeth. It points its ears to the front and stares at the person it is angry with. If a dog does this to you, don't go near it.

Staying healthy

Watch out for signs of your dog looking scruffy or not wanting to eat. If you think your dog is ill, look in your telephone directory for a vet near you.

When you first get your puppy, take it to a vet to check that it is healthy. After that, you will need to take your dog to a vet every year for a check-up.

Going to the vet

If your dog is ill, make an appointment to see a vet. Keep your dog warm and in a quiet place so that it can rest.

There will be lots of other animals at the vet's, so you will need to keep your dog on its leash until you see the vet.

Fleas tickle a dog's skin and make it scratch, like this puppy.

Watch out for your dog scratching a lot.

Fleas

If your dog scratches a lot, it may have tiny creatures called fleas, living in its fur. Ask the vet for advice on getting rid of fleas. The vet will sell you a special spray, drops or pills to kill the fleas.

Worms

Roundworms and tapeworms live in your dog's stomach and can make it very ill. If your dog has worms, it might eat more but lose weight at the same time. A vet will sell you pills for your dog, to protect it against both types of worms. Ask the vet how often your dog needs these pills.

Growing up

Your puppy must have some injections against diseases before it can go out for a walk. It will need another injection every year to keep it protected.

The vet will look at your dog's eyes and teeth too.

From six months old, your puppy can have a small operation to stop it from having puppies, or being the father of puppies. Ask a vet for advice.

Getting older

Some dogs live for ten years or longer. As your dog gets older, it will not run as far or as fast as it used to. Take it for shorter walks. It may want to sleep more, so make sure your dog's bed is in a warm place. Help your dog to keep clean by brushing it regularly.

Starting training

Training your dog will help you to look after it safely. Start to train your dog as soon as you get it so that it will get to know that you are the boss. Your puppy will need to know when it has done something right or wrong.

Good dog

Give your dog something it likes when it does what you want it to. You could give it a food treat, play a game with it or stroke it. Never hit your dog if it does something it shouldn't.

Say "good dog" as soon as your dog sits when you ask it to.

Training to sit

One of the first things to teach your puppy is to sit when you tell it to. Getting your dog to sit is a good way of calming it down if it gets too boisterous and jumps up.

You could use a dog biscuit as a treat.

Hold a small treat just above your dog's nose. As your dog looks up at the treat, it will begin to sit down.

As your dog sits down, say "sit" and give it a treat. Praise your dog to let it know that it has been good.

For a link to a website where you can watch a
cartoon about teaching your dog to sit, go to
www.usborne-quicklinks.com

Chewing things

Your puppy's teeth may ache as they grow. Chewing things helps them feel more comfortable. Older dogs like to chew things too. Some dogs chew things when they are bored, so make sure your dog always has something that it is allowed to chew.

If you see your dog chewing something it shouldn't, say "No!" in a firm voice. Give it a dog toy or special chew instead.

A dog toy like this one, is safe for a puppy to chew.

Puppy school

A puppy school will help you to train your dog to be obedient.

It is a good idea to take your dog to a training class, as well as training it at home. Your dog will also get used to meeting other dogs at the class.

To find out about classes near you, go to a vet and look for details on their notice board, or look up "dog training" in a telephone directory.

Before you go out

While your puppy is still having its injections and cannot go out, begin to get it used to walking on a leash. As your puppy starts to go out for walks, it will meet other dogs. So, it is a good idea to get it used to meeting other puppies while it is still young.

Hold the leash up out of your dog's way as you walk.

Practise walking with your dog around your house for a few minutes every day.

On the leash

Tell your dog to sit first.

Try turning corners and walking in a wavy line.

Give your dog a treat when it has walked well.

Clip your dog's leash onto the ring on its collar. Hold a treat by your side and let your dog sniff it, but don't give it the treat yet.

Start to walk along with your dog. As your dog walks by your side, say "heel". Let it sniff the treat as it walks.

If your dog wanders away from your side, remind it that you have a treat in your hand. Say "heel" when it comes back to your side.

For a link to a website where you can print out and shade in pictures of dogs and find lots of fun dog facts, go to **www.usborne-quicklinks.com**

Pulling

When you are walking, keep the leash loose between you and your dog. Hold a treat in the hand without the leash. If your dog pulls, show it the treat to tempt it back to your side.

Don't pull on the leash as you might hurt your dog's neck.

Buying a leash

You will need to buy a strong nylon or leather leash that is at least 1m (1 yard) long. When your dog is older, you could buy it an extending leash. This lets your dog explore farther while it is walking with you. Only use this when you are away from roads.

Puppy parties

When your puppy has had its injections, it cannot meet other dogs for a while, but it can meet puppies of the same age. Some vets have parties where puppies can meet.

The puppies get used to other dogs so that they are not scared or nervous when they are allowed out. Ask a vet about "puppy parties" near you.

Going for a walk

You will need to take your dog for a walk at least twice every day. Try to go to a place where your dog can run safely off the leash. Keep your dog on its leash for the first few walks even in a safe place, so that it gets used to its surroundings.

When you take your dog for a walk, don't let it go to the toilet where people walk. Parks often have a special area where dogs can go to the toilet. Clear up any mess that your dog makes. Take a scoop or an old spade and a plastic bag with you. Wash your hands as soon as you get home.

Work out a couple of different routes to make your walks more interesting.

Road sense

Before you cross a road, tell your puppy to sit. Wait until it is safe to cross and then walk across the road. Always keep your puppy on its leash while crossing and walking by roads.

Calling your puppy

Call your puppy's name to get its attention.

Ask a friend to hold your puppy by its collar, a small distance away. Show a treat to your puppy.

Crouch down and spread your arms wide to show your puppy that you want it to come to you.

As your puppy runs to you, say "come!" as it gets near. Give your puppy a treat and praise it.

On the scent

If your dog scratches the ground, it is leaving its scent behind.

A dog usually has an area that it treats as its own, called its territory. A dog marks its territory with its scent. It can smell which other animals have been there too.

A dog uses scent glands on its paws, neck and near its bottom to mark its territory. It goes to the toilet, rubs against things or scratches the ground to leave its scent.

Park games

Take a dog toy, such as a ball, with you when you exercise your dog. When you reach a safe area away from roads, such as a park, let your dog chase after the toy.

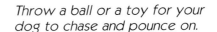

Throw a ball or a toy for your dog to chase and pounce on.

Never throw sticks for your dog. It could run into them and hurt itself as it tries to catch them.

Out and about

When you take your puppy for a walk, you will meet other dogs. It is important that your puppy knows how it should behave with other dogs. Most dogs will be friendly to puppies and play with them.

You might meet other people on your walks, too. Make sure that your puppy knows how it should behave with other people. Train your puppy not to jump up at them.

Meeting other dogs

When two dogs meet, they sniff each other all over. They identify other dogs by smell rather than sight.

Keep your dog on its leash.

If you think that a dog wants to fight, turn your dog's head away from the other dog and walk off.

Who is the strongest?

If one dog has a toy, it might shake it at the other dog to ask it to play.

You can buy a strong pulling toy for your dog from a pet store.

Dogs might growl as they pull a toy, but they are only pretending to be angry.

Sometimes dogs play tug of war to find out which one of them is the strongest. It is best if two dogs play this game. If you play, your dog might pull you over or you might hurt its teeth. Dogs with strong jaws, such as terriers, particularly like this game. If your dog likes playing tug of war, take a pulling toy on your walks.

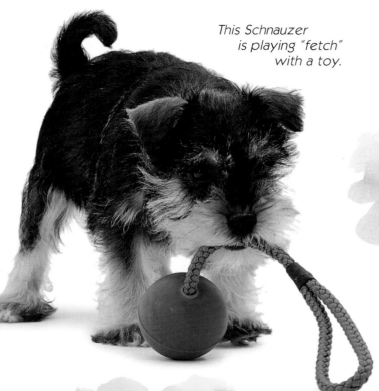

This Schnauzer is playing "fetch" with a toy.

Fetch

Use a soft toy that will not hurt your puppy's mouth.

Play "fetch" with your puppy. Show it a toy and let it sniff it. Throw the toy a short distance and say "fetch". When your puppy brings it back, take the toy away and praise your puppy.

Jumping up

Ignore your puppy if it jumps up.

Train your puppy at home not to jump up at people. If it jumps up at you, stand still and look away. If you try to push your puppy down or scold it when it jumps up, it might think that you are playing.

Your dog might jump up to try to lick your face to say "hello".

Your dog will jump up when it wants attention. Train it not to do this.

Brushing

You will need to brush your dog to keep its fur free of tangles and loose hair. Start brushing your puppy while it is still young, so that it gets used to it. Make sure you brush your dog before you give it a bath, or the tangles in its fur will get worse.

Dog brushes

A dog comb.

A carder pulls out dead fur.

A bristle brush is useful for long and short fur.

You will need a special brush and comb for your dog. There are different brushes for different fur types. Ask at a pet store which type you should use on your dog.

This Shi-tzu has thick, long fur. Fur like this needs to be brushed several times a week.

Smooth-haired dogs need to be brushed once a week.

Long fur needs to be brushed at least twice a week.

Wiry fur like this Schnauzer's, needs to be brushed twice a week.

For a link to a website where you can pick up some
good tips about grooming your dog, go to
www.usborne-quicklinks.com

Brushing your dog

It doesn't matter if your dog stands or sits.

Be careful not to tug and pull out any fur.

Some dogs love to have their stomachs brushed.

Spread newspaper on the floor for your dog to stand on. This will catch any fur and dirt that you brush out.

Start by brushing your dog's back. Brush the fur gently, in the direction that it grows.

Brush its legs, stomach and tail. Brush around your dog's ears and under its chin, too.

Shedding

Twice a year, most dogs shed a lot of their fur and grow a new coat. When your dog is shedding, brush it every day. Some dogs shed a little of their fur all year round.

Some curly-haired dogs don't shed at all. Like your hair, their fur keeps on growing. If your dog has fur like this, take it to a dog groomer to have its fur trimmed.

Bathing

Dogs lick their fur to try to keep clean. If your dog gets muddy, you can often brush the dirt out once it has dried. You will need to give your dog a bath when it gets very dirty or smelly. Otherwise, bath it every four to six months. You will need to wear old clothes and an apron, because you might get very wet. Buy dog shampoo from a vet or pet store and have an old towel ready to dry your dog.

Bathing your dog

Get someone to hold your dog by the collar.

Run about 7cm (3 inches) of warm water in a bathtub. Take care that the water is not too hot. Get someone to help you put your dog into the bathtub.

Ask someone to hold your dog steady while you wash it. Use a plastic jug to scoop up the water and wet your dog's body. Keep its head dry at this stage.

Don't rub shampoo into your dog's head.

Pour some shampoo into your hand and rub it into your dog's fur. Use your fingertips to rub it in. Make sure it gets right down to your dog's skin.

Rinse the shampoo out of your dog's fur with lots of warm water. Use a sponge or an old cloth to wet your dog's head and wipe it clean.

For a link to a website where you
can send a doggy ecard, go to
www.usborne-quicklinks.com

Drying off

Your dog might shake itself to get rid of a lot of the water in its fur. Let it do this before it gets out of the bath. Rub your dog all over with an old towel to get it dry.

Keep your dog inside while it is wet so that it does not get cold. While your dog is still wet, its fur does not keep it warm.

Keep an old towel just to use on your dog.

Smelly again

After a bath, it may seem strange to your dog to be without its usual dog smell. Some dogs cover themselves with strong smells to disguise themselves from other animals. For the first few days after you have given your dog a bath, watch out for your dog trying to roll in smelly things.

Going away

If you go away overnight, you will need someone to look after your dog. It will need to be fed, given water and exercised every day. Your dog will prefer to go with you, when you go away. Most dogs like to explore new places, but it's best not to take your puppy away from home until it has had its injections. Never leave your dog alone overnight. It may get bored and lonely without you.

Your dog may be nervous or excited by all the sights, sounds and smells of a new place.

Boarding kennels

If you cannot take your dog with you when you go away, it could stay in boarding kennels. Take some of your dog's toys and its bed to the kennels.

Your dog will feel more at home with its own things around it.

People at the kennels will look after your dog and take it for walks. Your dog must be at least six months old before it can stay in boarding kennels.

A change of scene

If your dog goes away with you, take all the things that it usually needs. Put the address of the place that you are staying in a plastic identity tag on your dog's collar. When you are in a new place, keep your dog near you, so it doesn't get lost.

Staying with friends

Put your friend's address on your dog's tag.

You may have a friend who can look after your dog while you are away. It's best only to let your dog stay with friends who know it well or have had dogs of their own.

Leave plenty of dog food with your friend and make sure they have the telephone number of your dog's vet, in case it is not well while you are away.

On the road

When your dog travels in a car, it can get very hot. Dogs cannot sweat to cool down, like people do, so keep a car window open, when your dog is inside. When you stop for a break, keep your dog on its leash and let it have a drink and go to the toilet.

Take your dog's water dish and a plastic bottle filled with water.

Give your dog some water in its dish when you stop.

INDEX